MODULORUM
IOANNIS MAILLARDI

RECENT RESEARCHES IN THE MUSIC OF THE RENAISSANCE

James Haar, general editor

A-R Editions, Inc., publishes seven series of musicological editions
that present music brought to light in the course of current research:

Recent Researches in the Music of the Middle Ages and Early Renaissance
Charles M. Atkinson, general editor

Recent Researches in the Music of the Renaissance
James Haar, general editor

Recent Researches in the Music of the Baroque Era
Christoph Wolff, general editor

Recent Researches in the Music of the Classical Era
Eugene K. Wolf, general editor

Recent Researches in the Music of the Nineteenth and Early Twentieth Centuries
Rufus Hallmark, general editor

Recent Researches in American Music
H. Wiley Hitchcock, general editor

Recent Researches in the Oral Traditions of Music
Philip V. Bohlman, general editor

Each *Recent Researches* edition is devoted to works
by a single composer or to a single genre of composition.
The contents are chosen for their potential interest to scholars
and performers, then prepared for publication according to the
standards that govern the making of all reliable historical editions.

Subscribers to any of these series, as well as patrons of subscribing institutions,
are invited to apply for information about the "Copyright-Sharing Policy"
of A-R Editions, Inc., under which policy any part of an edition
may be reproduced free of charge for study or performance.

Address correspondence to

A-R EDITIONS, INC.
801 Deming Way
Madison, Wisconsin 53717

(608) 836-9000

Jean Maillard

MODULORUM IOANNIS MAILLARDI

The Five-, Six-, and Seven-Part Motets

Part I

Edited by Raymond H. Rosenstock

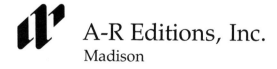 A-R Editions, Inc.

Madison

In memory of my dear brother
Henry M. Rosenstock
1928–83

© 1993 by A-R Editions, Inc.
All Rights Reserved
Printed in the United States of America

Library of Congress Cataloging-in-Publication Data

Maillard, Jean, fl. 1538–1572.
    [Moduli. Selections]
    Modulorum Ioannis Maillardi : the five-, six-, and seven-part
motets / Jean Maillard ; edited by Raymond H. Rosenstock.
        p.   cm. — (Recent researches in the music of the Renaissance,
ISSN 0486-123X ; v. 95–96)
    Words in Latin, also printed as texts with English translations;
pref. and critical notes in English.
    Edited from the 1st ed. (Paris : Le Roy & Ballard, 1565).
    Includes bibliographical references.
    ISBN 0-89579-280-X
    1. Motets.   I. Rosenstock, Raymond Hugh, 1938– .   II. Title.
III. Series.
M2.R2384 vol. 95–96   93-11486
                                                                    CIP
                                                                     M

Contents

Part I

Abbreviations

AM	*Antiphonale monasticum pro diurnis horis.* Tournai: Desclée, 1934.
AS	*Antiphonale Sarisburiense.* Edited by W. H. Frere. 2 vols. London: Plainsong and Mediaeval Music Society, 1901–25.
Divine Office	*The Hours of the Divine Office in English and Latin.* 3 vols. Collegeville, MN: Liturgical Press, 1963.
LR	*Liber responsorialis pro festis I. classis.* Solesmes: E Typographeo Sancti Petri, 1895.
LRB	François Lesure and Geneviève Thibault. *Bibliographie des éditions d'Adrian le Roy et Robert Ballard (1551–1598).* Paris: Heugel, 1955.
LU	*The Liber Usualis with Introduction and Rubrics in English.* New York: Desclée, 1956.
RRMR 73	Jean Maillard. *Modulorum Ioannis Maillardi . . . : The Four-Part Motets.* Edited by Raymond H. Rosenstock. Recent Researches in the Music of the Renaissance, 73. Madison: A-R Editions, 1987.
PM	*Processionale monasticum ad usum congregationis Gallicae.* Solesmes: E Typographeo Sancti Petri, 1893.
RISM	François Lesure. *Recueils imprimés, XVIe–XVIIe siècles: liste chronologique.* Répertoire international des sources musicales, series BI, vol. 1. Munich and Duisburg: G. Henle, 1960.
WA	*Antiphonaire monastique, XIIIe siècle: Codex F. 160 de la bibliothèque de la cathédrale de Worcester.* Paléographie musicale 12. Tournai: Desclée, 1922.

Preface

By far the largest collection of Maillard's sacred works is the *Modulorum Ioannis Maillardi,* published in two volumes by Le Roy and Ballard in Paris in 1565 (see plate 1). The first volume, dedicated to the fifteen-year-old Charles IX, contains thirty-seven motets, and the second, dedicated to the Queen Mother Catherine de' Medici, contains twenty-four additional motets and a set of Lamentations. RRMR 73 contains the four-voice motets from that set (eleven from each of the original volumes), and the current volume prints the remainder, thirty-nine motets for five to seven voices. As noted in RRMR 73, this Parisian collection from 1565 plus twenty-two motets found almost exclusively in a manuscript in Barcelona together account for practically all of Maillard's eighty-six known works in that genre. For information of a more general nature concerning the composer and his works and a detailed commentary on the four-voice motets, see the Preface of RRMR 73.

The Music of the Edition

Isabelle Cazeaux has rightfully called attention to a striking feature of Jean Maillard's religious music as compared to that of many of his French contemporaries: the ingenious treatment of cantus firmus technique.[1] Indeed, nowhere is this trait more in evidence than in the motets of LRB 96 and 97 printed in the present edition.

A particularly interesting example of Maillard's cantus firmus treatment is found in [19] "Fratres mei elongaverunt," in which the canon, which requires two resolutions (one in diminution and the other in augmentation, both of which are supplied in the principal source), is appropriate to the quotation from John 3:30 supplied therewith: "He must increase, but I must decrease." In addition, six other motets in LRB 96 and 97 have independent cantus firmus melodies presented in ostinato fashion: [5] "Exaudi Domine," in which the main melody of Josquin's *Faulte d'argent* is stated seven times as an ostinato (in the principal source, the associated text underlay does not appear, though it does appear elsewhere); [6] "Derelinquat impius," in which the cantus firmus, "Adjuva nos Deus," from verse 2 of the tract *Domine non secundum peccata nostra* for Ash Wednesday (as it appears in *LU,* 527), is stated four times, with eight measures of rests preceding each statement (see plate 2); [12] "Heu michi, Domine," in which the separate text "Parce michi Domine" is stated seven times, in long notes preceded by seven measures of rests before each appear-

ance in this motet in responsory form; [21] "Vidit Dominus," whose cantus firmus pattern occurs in four statements with various degrees of uneven augmentation and with two breves' worth of rests separating statements (plate 3); [27] "Ave Maria [I]," in which the independent chant segment "Ave, Maria, gratia plena," a more ornate variant of *LU,* 1861, is stated three times in the quinta voice (the second statement is transposed, intact, up a fourth, and the third is at the original pitch level and presented in somewhat uneven augmentation); [34] "Inviolata, integra," a most special case, in which four voices of this variation-chain sequence engage in a combination of paraphrase and migrating cantus-firmus treatment, while the fifth voice presents a chant segment, "Ave Maria, gratia plena," perhaps a litany of the Blessed Virgin Mary similar to *LU,* 836, fifteen times in ever-changing rhythmic guises in the top register (see plate 4). Could this work have influenced Monteverdi's strikingly similar *Sonata sopra Sancta Maria* of 1610?

Other ingenious cantus firmus treatments occur in the following motets: [18] "De fructu vitae," which requires finding the correct note values and rests for a cryptic melodic line that is supplied as a canonic puzzle (fortunately, the *resolutio* is also supplied; see plate 5); [22] "Surrexit Dominus," which more simply presents its tenor, a variant of the short responsory in *LU,* 244, in plainsong notation and, in common with [6] "Derelinquat impius," uses the cantus planus principle of even note values in which ligatures bear no rhythmic connotations.

In RRMR 73, the full range of text expression available to Maillard without the constraints of either cantus firmus treatment or of writing for more than four voices is evident. In the present volume, in which contrapuntal artifices abound, good examples of word painting are by no means absent, but are fewer and restricted mainly to the freely composed motets (and occasionally to those employing paraphrase) rather than those employing strict cantus firmus treatment. An exception is the aforementioned symbolic musical treatment of the text of [19] "Fratres mei elongaverunt," which features canon in augmentation and diminution.

Good examples of text expression do occur in such freely composed motets as [10] "In principio erat Verbum," in the *tertia pars* of which, just before "et Verbum caro factum est" (where the *Divine Office* calls for kneeling), rhythm is used in a manner reminiscent of Josquin's sacred works: the phrasing implies $\frac{3}{4}$ time in transcription, the bass line has three long notes that cut across the prevailing tactus, and the superius has a ligature that implies $\frac{3}{2}$ time in transcription. Whether or not religious numeric symbolism is present, one's attention is at the very least riveted to the text by the confluence of rhythmic details at that point.[2]

As one might therefore expect, [16] "Verbum caro factum est," an extended responsory in form (though freely composed), also provides examples of text expression, such as the possible numerical symbolism in the placement of the entries in measures 3, 7, and 9, and the idea of grace expressed in an extended tenor passage in minims in measure 44. Furthermore, the *secunda pars* begins with a trio and withholds the remaining two voices for twenty-three measures, till the Lord's glory is seen.

Other examples are not lacking. [14] "Victimae paschali laudes," which combines cantus firmus segments (*LU*, 780) with paraphrase, expresses the image of rising in comparatively high entries; it sets the text concerning resurrection for high voices, while the text concerning the tomb is set for low voices, and the major mode appears for the text "viventis." Another example is the long, stately note values for "magni consilii" in [37] "Puer natus est," measures 53–59. The declamatory quality of "Propter nomen tuum, Domine" (m. 50) stands out in the *prima pars* of [7] "Eripe me." Implied triple meter is used to good symbolic advantage in [28] "Ave, Maria [II]," measure 37. Plangent fourths occur in the darkly dramatic (and motivically organized) [32] "O crux benedicta," measures 71–72. Quite a wide melodic range can be found for the text "universa multitudo" in measure 25 of [23] "Decantabat populus Israël." Similarly, there is an extravagant ascent in measures 8–10, contratenor, of [39] "Hodie Maria virgo," a paraphrase setting (*LU*, 1607), whose high tessitura (especially for "exaltata") and bright F-Ionian mode express a joyous final salutation to the Queen Mother (Catherine de' Medici, the dedicatee of LRB 97).

On a more speculative level in the realm of text expression, perhaps the very use of such a text as "Have I been so long a time with you, and you have not known me" in [9] "Domine ostende nobis Patrem" is to be taken as a rather cryptic personal plea on the part of Maillard for recognition. The placement of [19] "Fratres mei elongaverunt" in the final position of LRB 16 invites further speculation along these lines.

To be sure, there is some sacrifice of ideal part writing in order to achieve the artifices that Maillard wished to display in the *Modulorum* of 1565, the collection of works representative of his best efforts. Thus, we have parallel fifths between superius and tenor in [6] "Derelinquat impius," measures 74 and 75, parallel octaves between superius and bass in [21]

"Vidit Dominus Petrum et Andream," measure 10, and even a rather abrupt cutoff in measures 24 and 59 of [35] "Diffusa est gratia" to avoid an awkward meeting between the A in the quinta pars voice with the G of the tenor on the following fractional beat. In addition, a few archaisms occur here and there, as in [7] "Eripe me," with *fauxbourdon* in the *secunda pars*, measure 44, and an under-third cadence in measure 59.

As noted in the discussion of the four-voice motets of LRB 97 (RRMR 73), four of those use unusually high clef combinations that commend the works for treble voices. In the present volume, eight more motets emphasize the higher registers: [27] "Ave, Maria [I]," [28] "Ave, Maria [II]," [29] "Deus, Deus meus," [30] "Ave, stella matutina," [34] "Inviolata, integra," [35] "Diffusa est gratia," [37] "Puer natus est," and [38] "Assumpta est Maria." These are all drawn from LRB 97, the volume dedicated to the Queen Mother.

The geographic dispersion and publishing history of a few of the motets in the present collection may serve as an index of the esteem in which Maillard was held in his day. Among these we may cite: [2] "Ascendo ad Patrem meum," which was also printed by Du Chemin in Paris (RISM 1554[7]), Du Bosc and Guéroult in Geneva (RISM 1554[12], 1556[10]), Berg and Neuber in Nuremberg (RISM 1555[10]), and Sylvius in Geneva (RISM [1559][5]), and appeared in manuscripts in Dresden (Sächsische Landesbibliothek, MS G1 5, dated 1583–84; Gri 56, 1568–85; Pi VIII, ca. 1560), Regensburg (Proske-Bibliothek, MS A.R. 877, dated 1572) and Zwickau (Ratsschulbibliothek, MS 11, ca. 1579–91?); the magisterial [26] "Gaudent in caelis," which was also printed by Berg and Neuber in Nuremberg (RISM 1564[2]) and appeared in manuscripts in Munich (Bayerische Staatsbibliothek, MS 132 II [Mus. Ms. 1536], dated 1583), Regensburg (Proske-Bibliothek, MS A.R. 795, dated 1572–77) and Zwickau (Ratsschulbibliothek, MS 11); and the equally magisterial [19] "Fratres me elongaverunt," which also appeared in a manuscript in Rome (Biblioteca Apostolica Vaticana, Cappella Sistina, MS 38, dated 1563). A lute arrangement of [8] "Domine, si tu es" was published as early as RISM 1551[24] in Paris (in Le Roy and Ballard's earliest publication) before appearing in print as a vocal motet. Furthermore, [1] "Laudate Dominum omnes gentes" was printed as late as RISM 1580[4] in Book II of Orlando di Lasso's *Theatri musici* in Geneva.

A few of Maillard's works inspired other composers of the Renaissance. Among the present motets, [7] "Eripe me" was parodied in a mass *a 5* by Palestrina (1582, in his *Missarum liber quartus*, Gardano, Rome), and [26] "Gaudent in caelis" seems to have been the basis for Orlando di Lasso's more modest setting *a 4* (1573, in his *Patrocinium Musices*, Munich).

Furthermore, perhaps Lesure is correct in his assertion, based on Lasso's apparent familiarity with Maillard's oeuvre, that resemblances between their *Exaudi Domine* settings are to be found (Maillard's setting *a 5* is [5] in the present edition, while that of Lasso, also *a 5*, was printed in his [25] *Sacrae cantiones*, Nuremberg (1562), and was based on a rather different text).[3]

The two distinctive sides of Maillard's skill, the expressive and the technical—we might even say the emotional and the intellectual, are amply represented in the collections of his motets published in RRMR 73 and the present volume. That these aspects of Maillard's musical personality are by no means mutually exclusive in his impressive works accrues to his stature as a composer of the mid-Renaissance, a *Kleinmeister* who provides an important link between the giants Josquin and Lassus.

Sources

The principal source for the present edition is Modulorum Ioannis Maillardi (Paris, 1565), in two volumes.

LRB 96 MODULORUM|IOANNIS MAILLARDI,| quaternis, quinis, senis, & septenis|vocibus modulatorum|PRIMUM VOLUMEN.|Apud Adrianum le Roy, & Robertum Ballard,|. . .|1565.|. . . The principal source for [1]–[26] of this edition, LRB 96 also contains eleven motets *a 4* (published in RRMR 73). The superius, tenor, and bassus partbooks for this source are preserved in Madrid, Biblioteca del Conservatorio, S. 3895 (4), 3896 (4), and 3899 (4), respectively. Partbooks for contratenor, tenor, and bassus survive in Paris, Bibliothèque Sainte-Geneviève, Rés. Vm. 76. The quinta and sexta partbook survives only in Chicago, Newberry Library, Case VM 2099/L1/K39.

LRB 97 MODULORUM|IOANNIS MAILLARDI| . . .|SECUNDUM VOLUMEN.|. . .|Apud Adrianum le Roy, & Robertum Ballard,|. . .|1565. The principal source for [27]–[39] of this edition, LRB 97 also contains eleven motets *a 4* (published in RRMR 73). The superius, tenor, and bassus partbooks for this source are preserved in Madrid, Biblioteca del Conservatorio, S. 3895 (5), 3896 (5), and 3899 (5), respectively. Partbooks for contratenor, tenor, and bassus survive in Paris, Bibliothèque Sainte-Geneviève, Rés. Vm. 77. The quinta and sexta partbook survives only in Chicago, Newberry Library, Case VM 2099/L1/K39.

More motets by Maillard are concentrated in LRB 96, 97 than in any other single place, and the accuracy of the notation is exemplary. Therefore, though extremely minor differences can be found in other sources, such as variants in the embellished melodic

figures at cadences or the use of minor coloration instead of dotted notes (or vice versa), the LRB 96, 97 readings are taken as definitive.

The following two prints, likewise issued by Le Roy and Ballard, have been consulted as supplementary sources for this edition. The eight motets by Maillard found in LRB 7 were reprinted in LRB 96, 97, as were the twenty motets by Maillard printed in LRB 16.

LRB 7 LIBER PRIMUS|SEXDECIM MUSICALES MODULOS . . . Apud Adrianum le Roy, & Robertum Ballard . . .|9 Ianuarij 1552 (= RISM 1553[7]N.S.). LRB 7 contains three Maillard motets *a 5* (numbers [5], [7], and [10]), one motet *a 6* ([38]), and one *a 7* ([26]), as well as three motets *a 4* published in RRMR 73 (none of these motets are in LRB 16). Partbooks for superius, contratenor, and tenor survive in Paris, Bibliothèque Nationale, Rés. Vm[1] 213; the bassus is lacking, and additional voice parts for some motets are interspersed within the already listed partbooks.

LRB 16 IOANNIS MAILLARD|MUSICI EXCELLENTISSIMI MOTETA,|quator, quinque, & sex vocum.|LIBER PRIMUS.|. . . Apud Adrianum le Roy, & Robertum Ballard . . .|1555. LRB 16 contains nine motets *a 5* ([1], [2], [3], [6], [8], [14], [17], [18], [37]), three *a 6* ([19], [22], [39]), as well as eight motets *a 4* published in RRMR 73. Partbooks for superius, contratenor, tenor, and bassus survive in Paris, Bibliothèque Nationale, Rés. Vm[1] 121; the quinta pars is lacking, and additional voice parts for some motets are interspersed within the already listed partbooks.

Editorial Methods

Original note values are reduced by half and modern barlines have been employed throughout the edition. Ligatures and coloration are indicated by ⌐ ¬ and ⌐ ¬, respectively. Incipits show the original clefs, key signs, mensurations, note values, and any initial rests. Ranges are indicated at the beginning of each piece, before the initial modern clefs.

The application of *musica ficta* (indicated above each note affected) has been guided by sixteenth-century conventions as follows: to avoid false relations; to avoid melodic tritones (whether direct or approached by scale steps followed by a change in melodic direction); to approach perfect consonances from the nearest imperfect consonances between the same two voices at cadences (i.e., make sixths major when followed by octaves, make thirds major before perfect fifths or unisons if the upper voice is rising by a step, and make thirds minor before perfect fifths if the upper voice is descending by a step); to lower a melodic whole step above *la* to a half step if followed by a return to *la* (where the maxim "una nota super *la,* semper est canendum *fa"* traditionally applies, especially in situations in which tritones would otherwise be outlined melodically; to make minor chords at the end of *partes* into major chords. In questionable circumstances, special attention has also been given to consistency of melodic (and even motivic) imitation, phrase repetition (and of course sectional repetition), and statements of a cantus prius factus. In some situations, it should be noted that Maillard seems to require one pattern of *musica ficta* when a phrase repeats at its original pitch level and another when the same phrase repeats at another pitch level (notably at the fifth), and that he then appears to stay consistent within each level. Lastly, a distinctly modern assumption of overall stylistic consistency of application has been made, and the editor takes full responsibility for that assumption.

Accidentals in parentheses above the staff are cautionary. Source sharps that serve to raise a flatted pitch have been rendered in the edition as naturals. Where an accidental as applied to a given pitch in the source is repeated within a single bar of the transcription, the modern convention in which accidentals are in effect for the duration of the measure has been observed.

Wherever possible, text repetitions are drawn from those in prints by Le Roy and Ballard (LRB); when *ij* occurs in LRB 96 or 97, angle brackets (⟨ ⟩) enclose the realized text repetition. (Occasionally, *ij* appears in LRB 16 where there is text in LRB 96 or 97, or vice versa; in all cases the resulting underlays are identical.) If text repetition is suggested by the editor, the resulting underlay is given within square brackets. For clarity of form, all lines of text are begun with a capital letter, whether or not this practice conforms with that in the original source or in modern chant books. End punctuation follows modern chant books wherever possible or the *Divine Office.* Spellings are as in LRB 96 and 97, with the following exceptions: ę has been transcribed as *ae,* *à* has become *a,* and, where appropriate, *v* has been rendered as *u.* A few spellings have been standardized to facilitate syllabification in keeping with word division in *LU.*

Critical Notes

The critical notes for each motet indicate the principal and supplementary sources for this edition, chant sources (for motets based in any way upon a cantus prius factus), and variants, occasionally with further comment. The folio numbers after the source sigla refer only to the superius partbooks.

The variants reported herein are intended to supplement the readings given in LRB 96 and 97, and, unless otherwise specified, they are readings in the secondary sources. The relatively few critical reports

given here are found in the "Comment" section of notes on individual pieces.

All pitches are reported in lowercase letters; other letters represent rhythmic values (L = longa, B = breve, SB = semibreve, M = minim, SM = semiminim, F = fusa; before any of these letters, d = dotted and c = coloration; lig = ligature). No attempt has been made to report the use of minor color for dotted note values. Voice parts are indicated as Sup, CT, Ten, Ba, Qu, and Se for superius, contratenor, tenor, bassus, quinta pars, and sexta pars, respectively. Variant text appears in italics.

[1] Laudate Dominum omnes gentes

Sources: LRB 96 (10r), LRB 16 (10v).

Variants: The Ba partbook of LRB 96 reverses the order of this and the following motet. In LRB 16, the Quinta Pars is called "Secundus Superius." M. 22, Ten, instead of notes 1 and 2, g (SB). M. 34, Sup, note 2 through m. 35, note 1, a–g–f (dM–SM–SB). M. 37, through m. 38, note 1, d–d (SB–dSB).

Chant Source: Psalm tone 5 (*LU,* 115).

Comment: This motet is also printed in RISM 1580[4] (Lassus); it is a paraphrase setting.

[2] Ascendo ad Patrem meum

Sources: LRB 96 (10v), LRB 16 (8r).

Variants: The Ba part book of LRB 96 reverses the order of this and the preceding motet. Sup is called "Primus Superius" in LRB 16, which lacks Qu, presumably called "Secundus Superius." M. 47, Sup, e-sharp [i.e., e-natural]. M. 82, Ba, no alleluia repetition.

Chant Source: For the *prima pars,* the antiphon at the Benediction on Ascension Day (*LU,* 845).

Comment: This motet is found in numerous other sources, including RISM 1554[7], 1554[12], 1555[10], 1556[10] [1559][5], Dresden MS G1 5 (ca. 1583/84), Dresden Gri 56 (ca. 1568–85), Dresden Pi VIII (ca. 1560, ascribed to "Meilart"), Regensburg MS 877 (1572), Zwickau MS 11 (ca. 1579–91?); it is a paraphrase setting.

[3] Si quis diligit me

Sources: LRB 96 (11v), LRB 16 (11v).

Variants: Sup called "Primus Superius" and Qu called "Secundus Superius" in LRB 16.

Comment: This motet is freely composed.

[4] Timete Dominum

Source: LRB 96 (12r).

Comment: This motet is freely composed.

[5] Exaudi Domine

Sources: LRB 96 (12v), LRB 7 (7r).

Variants: Qu, in Ten book of LRB 7, quotes Josquin's tune the first time with Latin text, with the French "Faute . . . pareille" below, and subsequent cantus firmus statements repeat only the French. Ten of LRB 7 is fairly unclear, and Ba is lacking. M. 61, Ten, notes 3 and 4 are given as one d (SB). M. 78, Sup, note 2, no sharp.

Comment: This motet is also printed in RISM 1559[1]. The cantus firmus appears as an ostinato in Qu. Perhaps this motet is the basis for a setting by Lasso (a 5, printed in 1562 in his [25] *Sacrae cantiones*, Nuremberg (1562), which is, however, based on a rather different text). For a modern edition of Lasso's motet, see *O. de Lassus: Sämtliche Werke*, ed. F. X. Haberl and A. Sandberger (Leipzig: Breitkopf & Härtel, 1894–1926), 7:158.

[6] *Derelinquat impius*

Sources: LRB 96 (13r), LRB 16 (12v).

Chant Source: Cantus firmus, "Adjuva nos Deus," is verse 2 of the tract "Domine non secundum peccata nostra" for Ash Wednesday (*LU*, 527).

Comment: In both sources, this motet has parallel fifths in mm. 74–75 between Ten and Sup.

[7] *Eripe me*

Sources: LRB 96 (13v), LRB 7 (5r).

Variants: Ten called "Primus Tenor" and Qu called "Secundus Tenor" in LRB 7; Ba lacking. *Secunda pars*—Mm. 66–67, Qu, e not flatted.

Comment: This motet is freely composed. It is parodied in a mass a 5 by Palestrina (1582, in his *Missarum liber quartus*, Gardano, Rome, published in *G. P. da Palestrina: Le opere complete*, ed. by R. Casimiri et al. (Rome: Edizione Fratelli Scalera, 1939–), 10:79.

[8] *Domine, si tu es*

Sources: LRB 96 (14v), LRB 16 (13r).

Variants: Ten called "Primus Tenor" and Qu called "Secundus Tenor" in LRB 16.

Comment: Note that the lute arrangement in RISM 1551[24] precedes the first printing of this work in its vocal form. This motet is cited by F. Lesure as a classic example of Maillard's melodic discontinuity.[4]

[9] *Domine ostende nobis Patrem*

Source: LRB 96 (15r).

Chant Source: Perhaps a loose variant of antiphons 1 and 2, second vespers for Saints Philip and James, 11 May (*LU*, 1465E).

Comment: This motet provides a good example of repeating bass phrases starting on the same pitch level, even to the point of a quasi ostinato in a threefold alleluia (mm. 29–34).

[10] *In principio erat Verbum*

Sources: LRB 96 (15v), LRB 7 (1v).

Variants: Ba lacking in LRB 7. Ten called "Secundus Tenor" in LRB 7 in first two sections, but is called "Primus Tenor" in the third section, whereas Qu is correspondingly called "Primus Tenor" and "Secundus Tenor." [*Prima pars*]—M. 105, Qu, fermata. *Secunda pars*—M. 74, Ten, notes 1 and 2 are a single b (SB). M. 80, Sup, g not sharped. *Tertia pars*—M. 40, Qu, given as g–a–g–g (M–dM–SM–SB). M. 63, Ten, note 2 erroneously g in LRB 7. M. 81, Qu, no lig, and from last note of m. 79 to last note of m. 81, e–d–d–c–d–g (dM–SM–SB–M–SB–SB). M. 119, CT, no sharp.

Chant Source: Perhaps a loose variant of responsories 11 and 12 for the Nativity of the Lord (*LR*, 66 and 67, or *WA*, 30)?

Comment: In this motet, there is a recurrent motivic kernel, (e)–g–a–c, as well as striking text symbolism. The text erroneously reads ". . . nihil. Quod factum . . ."

[11] *O Rex gloriae*

Source: LRB 96 (18v).

Chant Source: Perhaps for [*Prima pars*], a loose variant of the antiphon at the magnificat of Sunday within the Octave of the Ascension (*WA*, 150 or *LU*, 853); the whole may be an unknown responsory and verse.

Comment: There is apparent paraphrase technique in this motet.

[12] *Heu michi, Domine*

Source: LRB 96 (18v).

Comment: In this piece, cantus firmus technique is applied to an unknown melody.

[13] *Congregati sunt inimici nostri*

Source: LRB 96 (19v).

Comment: Freely composed.

[14] *Victimae paschali laudes*

Sources: LRB 96 (20r), LRB 16 (7v).

Variants: Sup called "Primus Superius" and Qu called "Secundus Superius" in LRB 16. Several inconsequential differences in coloration of dotted note values. [*Prima pars*]—M. 77, CT, e-sharp [i.e., e-natural]. *Secunda pars*—M. 23, CT, note 4 given as f–e (F–F) and m. 24, note 2 is given as e–d (cSB–M). M. 27, CT, note 4 to m. 28 note 1 is a–g (dM–SM). M. 39, CT, note 4 is e–e (M–M). M. 39, Ten, for beats 1 and 2, c–b-flat–a (dM–2F). M. 50, CT, note 4 to m. 51 note 1 is a–g (dM–SM). M. 74, CT, note 2 is e–d (F–F). M. 80, CT, note 1 is d–e (dM–SM). M. 95, Ba is d–d (2SB).

Chant Source: Sequence for Easter Sunday (*LU*, 780), slight variant.

Comment: A modern edition of this motet appears in J. Heywood Alexander, ed., *Moduli Undecim Festorum*, Recent Researches in the Music of the Renaissance, 56 (Madison: A-R Editions, 1983). Both migrating cantus firmus and paraphrase techniques are combined. In addition, this piece contains madrigalisms and text symbolism. The overall tessitura of the piece is high.

[15] Omnes gentes attendite

Source: LRB 96 (21r).

Comment: This piece is also printed in RISM 1551[1], 1555[6].

[16] Verbum caro factum est

Source: LRB 96 (21v).

Comment: This motet is freely composed and contains motivic treatment of the opening materials; the final line is musically repeated as in a Parisian chanson. The overall form of the piece suggests an extended responsory.

[17] Nunc dimittis servum tuum

Sources: LRB 96 (23r), LRB 16 (14r).

Variants: Ten called "Primus Tenor" and Qu called "Secundus Tenor" in LRB 16.

Chant Source: Antiphon and canticle at the Blessing of the Candles for the Purification of the Blessed Virgin Mary (LU, 1357).

Comment: This motet combines migrating cantus firmus and paraphrase techniques; it also contains the archaism of an under-third cadence in m. 58, Qu, "Lumen ad revelationem," which is perhaps used symbolically.

[18] De fructu vitae

Sources: LRB 96 (23v), LRB 16 (6v).

Variants: Qu gives the canon, but omits the resolutio (the latter is lacking in LRB 16).

Comment: The cantus firmus, "Fiat Domine cor meum," is an unknown melody (see [19] "Cantantibus organis" in RRMR 73. The "Canon: Tout vient a poinct qui scait attendre," in both sources, requires finding the correct note values and rests for the cryptic melody supplied.

[19] Fratres mei elongaverunt

Sources: LRB 96 (24r), LRB 16 (16r).

Variants: Sup called "Primus Superius" and Qu called "Secundus Superius" in LRB 16.

Comment: Ten, in both sources, carries the following instruction "Canon. Me oportet minui: Illum autem crescere." Qu of LRB 96 carries the instruction "Resolutio minuentis," and gives a transcription of Qu at the reduction of the present edition; also, "Resolutio crescentis" gives the entire voice line at note values corresponding to those actually adopted for the transcription of Ten in this edition (and that reading is used only for the first several notes before the end of the motet is reached). Thus, the ratio of notevalues between Ten and Qu is 1:4 in this mensuration canon. (Perhaps the placement of this motet as the final piece of LRB 16 has some autobiographical significance in symbolic form?) This motet also appears in Rome MS 38.

[20] Ecce venit ad templum

Source: LRB 96 (24v).

Chant Source: Invitatory for the Purification of the Blessed Virgin Mary, matins, 2 February (LR, 433).

Comment: The recurring motive d–f–d is drawn from the opening of the chant.

[21] Vidit Dominus Petrum et Andream

Source: LRB 96 (25r).

Comment: The cantus firmus, an unknown melody, appears four times, with uneven augmentation; parallel octaves occur between Sup and Ba in m. 10.

[22] Surrexit Dominus vere

Sources: LRB 96 (25v), LRB 16 (15v).

Variants: Qu called "Secundus Bassus" in the Ten book of LRB 16.

Chant Source: The resolutio is a variant of the short responsory for Easter Sunday, sext (LU, 244).

Comment: The resolutio, in Sup book of LRB 96, is given as Se in the present transcription. The chant is in even breves. The instruction "Canon in diapenthe" (which is puzzling) and commentary "Dum tempus habemus, operemus bonum" appear in the Sup book of both sources.

[23] Decantabat populus Israël

Source: LRB 96 (26v).

Comment: 2a Ba is in the Sup book. This motet is in responsory form, and is possibly freely composed.

[24] Estote ergo misericordes

Source: LRB 96 (27v).

Comment: This motet is a freely composed responsory.

[25] In pace

Source: LRB 96 (28r).

Chant Source: Responsory and verse (AS I, 150).

Comment: In this motet, paraphrase technique is employed. The text "somnum" is spelled "sumnum" in all voices. Secunda and tertia partes are textually continuous, with no grammatical break.

[26] Gaudent in caelis

Sources: LRB 96 (28v), LRB 7 (7v).

Variants: Qu called "Secunda Superius," Ten called "Primus Tenor," and Se called "Secundus Tenor" in LRB 7.

Chant Source: Antiphon for the Common Commemoration of Saints (with a minor text variant, combining musical features of LU, 262; AM, 653; and WA, 351).

Comment: This motet combines cantus firmus and paraphrase techniques. As described above, this impressive tour de force also appears in RISM 1553[7], 1564[2], Munich Mus. Ms. 1536 (dated 1583); Regensburg MS 795 (dated 1572–77); and Zwickau MS 11 (ca. 1579–91?). This motet appears to be the basis for a setting *a 4* by Lassus in his *Patrocinium musices*, Munich, 1573. For a modern edition of that work, see *O. de Lassus: Sämtliche Werke*, ed. F. X. Haberl and A. Sandberger (Leipzig: Breitkopf & Härtel, 1894–1926), 1:133.

[27] *Ave, Maria [I]*

Source: LRB 97 (12r).

Chant Source: Marian antiphon (*LU*, 1861), variant.

Comment: The cantus firmus in Qu is stated three times; in the second statement, it is transposed up a fourth, and in the third statement it comes back down to pitch and appears in somewhat uneven augmentation. The overall tessitura of the piece is high.

[28] *Ave, Maria [II]*

Source: LRB 97 (12v).

Chant Source: Perhaps the Marian antiphon at the second vespers for 25 March (*LU*, 1416), treated as a loose fantasia.

[29] *Deus, Deus meus*

Source: LRB 97 (13r).

Comment: This motet seems to be freely composed, with only the most tenuous resemblances to the offertory for the second Sunday after Easter (*LU*, 818). It resembles the previous piece, with ending materials in an idiom suggestive of Maillard's "Cantantibus organis" (see [19] in RRMR 73).

[30] *Ave, stella matutina*

Source: LRB 97 (13v).

Chant Source: Antiphon for the Blessed Virgin Mary (*PM*, 277), expanded and in mode 1 instead of 7.

Comment: [*Prima Pars*]—Mm. 49–50, Sup, "clipeum." Mm. 53–54, Ba, "tue." Mm. 62–64, Ba, "virgua." Mm. 78–81, Sup, "amyngdalum." In this piece both cantus firmus and paraphrase techniques are combined; solmization for the text "solare" is employed. Chevalier lists the text as no. 2134, and erroneously dates it ca. 1583.[5]

[31] *Tota pulchra es*

Source: LRB 97 (14v).

Comment: This motet appears to be freely composed, and is probably unrelated melodically to the antiphon in honor of the Blessed Virgin Mary (*WA*, 360); there is end repetition as in a Parisian chanson. The unknown melody in Sup, mm. 38–43, repeats in strophic fashion in mm. 44–50.

[32] *O crux benedicta*

Source: LRB 97 (15v).

Comment: This motet is freely composed (*WA*, 308 has a similar text) and contains many expressive madrigalisms.

[33] *Regina coeli*

Source: LRB 97 (16v).

Chant Source: Marian antiphon for Sunday at compline (the closest match is the chant supplied for a setting *a 4* by Maillard in Barcelona MS 682; see RRMR 73, p. xiii).

Comment: In this motet, cantus firmus and paraphrase techniques are combined.

[34] *Inviolata, integra*

Source: LRB 97 (17v).

Chant Source: Sequence in honor of the Blessed Virgin Mary (*LU*, 1861), variant. Cantus firmus, "Ave, Maria, gratia plena," Litany of the Blessed Virgin Mary (*LU*, 836), variant.

Comment: The cantus firmus, stated fifteen times, recurs in ever-changing rhythmic guises, anticipating Monteverdi's *Sonata sopra Sancta Maria*. A variation-chain sequence. In mm. 78–82, Ba, and mm. 83–87, Sup, "dulcis sona" is found in LRB 97 rather than "dulcisona," found in the other voices. Qu is marked "QUINTA PARS DE INVIOLATA." The cantus firmus is often the highest sounding voice; overall, the tessitura is high. Since Qu consistently sounds above Sup when they are simultaneously active, Qu has been printed on top in the present edition.

[35] *Diffusa est gratia*

Source: LRB 97 (19r).

Comment: This motet is freely composed and is in the responsory form aBcB, in which the a and c sections bear some mutual musical resemblances. The editorial $\frac{3}{2}$ meter of m. 51 provides a smooth transition to the (somewhat varied) B section in its original metric orientation.

[36] *Stemmata maiorum*

Source: LRB 97 (19r).

Comment: This motet is freely composed, loosely based on a melody first presented in aa'bb' form. The text, unknown, is perhaps addressed to Catherine de' Medici, the Queen Mother.

[37] *Puer natus est*

Sources: LRB 97 (19v), LRB 16 (13v).

Variants: Ba, m. 62 erroneously has neither text nor implied repetition.

Chant Source: Introit for the third Mass of the Nativity (*LU*, 408; very similar to the chant given for his setting *a 4*, which appears only in Barcelona MS 682).

Comment: This motet combines cantus planus setting of the cantus firmus in Qu (using many ligatures; a purposeful archaism?) with paraphrase in the other voices.

[38] *Assumpta est Maria*

Sources: LRB 97 (20r), LRB 7 (8v).

Variants: Sup called "Primus Superius," Qu called "Secundus Superius," and Se called "Secundus Tenor" in LRB 7. CT of LRB 7 has bleed through, and thus some obscure areas; it correctly gives m. 48 as a–a–b, where LRB 97 erroneously has a–b–b. M. 71, Sup, last note and tie is sharped in LRB 7.

Chant Source: Antiphon at second vespers for 15 August (*LU*, 1605), variant.

Comment: This motet is a paraphrase setting in A(A)BA form. Two text verses are skipped, but the musical continuity precludes any *alternatim* performance.

[39] *Hodie Maria virgo*

Sources: LRB 97 (20v), LRB 16 (14v).

Variants: Sup called "Primus Superius," Qu called "Secundus Superius," Ten called "Primus Tenor," and Se called "Secundus Tenor" in LRB 16. M. 34, Ten, notes 2 and 3 are given as f (dM) in LRB 7.

Chant Source: Conflation of the antiphon "Hodie" and the versicle and response "Exaltata est" for the Assumption of the Blessed Virgin Mary, 15 August, first and second vespers (*LU*, 1607; see also the variant *WA*, 360).

Comment: This motet is a paraphrase by simplification. There is an extravagant ascent in mm. 8–10, CT, for the opening text. The tops of vocal ranges are featured in mm. 47–55 in Sup and CT for the text "Exaltata est sancta Dei Genetrix." LRB has "Exaltata es" in all voices.

Acknowledgments

For the provision of the microfilms needed to transcribe these motets, I am indebted to Paris, Bibliothèque Nationale (for Rés. Vm¹ 213, LRB 7, and Rés. Vm¹ 121, LRB 16, and where Bibliothèque Sainte-Geneviève, Rés. Vm. 76 and 77, LRB 96 and 97, with the exception of the missing Quinta and Sexta voice partbook, were processed). The only surviving copy of the Quinta and Sexta voice partbook known to me is in the collection of the Newberry Library in Chicago, in Case VM 2099/L1/K39, as listed by Donald W. Krummel in his *Bibliographical Inventory to the Early Music in the Newberry Library* (Boston: G. K. Hall, 1977); I would like to thank librarian Anthony Amodeo, according to whom it was acquired into the collection in 1961, and most especially François Lesure, who informed me of the existence of that copy several years ago when I had despaired of locating one after several false leads. (The copy in Madrid inventoried by Lesure and Thibault in their LRB catalogue has vanished; another in Treviso has perished with some 70,000 volumes during the bombing raid of 7 April 1944, according to a letter kindly sent me by library director Mons. Angelo Campagner.) Professor Charles H. Sherman of the University of Missouri at Columbia generously lent me his photo copy of the surviving source for use during my dissertation years. My remaining debts of gratitude are listed in the corresponding section of RRMR 73, with one important exception: I wish at this point to thank the administration and sabbatical committee of Keene State College, who granted me the leaves that made possible most of the work on these volumes of motets by Jean Maillard. Any remaining oversights and errors that may have passed the watchful eyes of my patient editors at A-R Editions are my own.

Notes

1. *The New Grove Dictionary of Music and Musicians*, s.v. "Maillard, Jean (i)."

2. For religiously symbolic applications of triple meter in Josquin's works, see Willem Elders, *Studien zur Symbolik in der Musik der alten Niederländer* (Bilthoven: A. B. Creyghton, 1968), especially pp. 30, 150, and 194.

3. Palestrina's mass is printed in *G. P. da Palestrina: Le opere complete*, ed. R. Casimiri et al. (Rome: Edizione Fratelli Scalera, 1939–), 10:79. The setting of "Gaudent in caelis" by Lassus is printed in *O. de Lassus: Sämtliche Werke*, ed. F. X. Haberl and A. Sandberger (Leipzig: Breitkopf & Härtel,

1894–1926), 1:133, while his setting in question (one of three) of "Exaudi Domine" appears in 7:158. Lesure's observations are offered in his article, "La Musique religieuse française au XVIe siècle," *Revue musicale* no. 222 (1953–54): 69.

4. *The New Oxford History of Music*, (London: Oxford University Press, 1968), 4:246.

5. Cyr Ulysse Chevalier, *Repertorium hymnologicum. Catalogue des chants, hymnes, proses, séquences, tropes.* (Brussels: Société des Bollandistes, 1892–1921; reprint, Hildesheim: Olms, 1971), 1:125.

Texts and Translations

The texts of the motets of LRB 96 and 97 are identified by biblical reference or liturgical reference or both. The liturgical references follow those given in Carl Marbach, *Carmina Scripturarum* (Straßburg, 1907; reprint, Hildesheim: Olms, 1963) and *The Hours of the Divine Office in English and Latin,* 3 vols. (Collegeville, Minn.: The Liturgical Press, 1963); the translations of certain liturgical texts are based on the latter work or on Dom Gaspar Lefebvre et al., *Saint Andrew Daily Missal* (Saint Paul, MN: E. M. Lohmann, 1961). Translations of scriptural texts are based on the Douay-Rheims version of the Holy Bible.

[1] Laudate Dominum, omnes gentes

Antiphon for Sunday at second vespers (from Psalm 116)

Laudate Dominum, omnes gentes,
Laudate eum omnes populi.
Quoniam confirmata est super nos misericordia eius,
Et veritas Domini manet in aeternum.

(O praise the Lord, all ye nations, praise him, all ye people. For his mercy is confirmed upon us, and the truth of the Lord remaineth for ever.)

[2] Ascendo ad Patrem meum

Antiphon text for the Benediction for the Ascension of Our Lord (from John 20:17), with an addition used as a verse in the responsory "Tempus est" for the same festival (from John 16:7)

Ascendo ad Patrem meum, et Patrem vestrum, alleluia,
Deum meum, et Deum vestrum, alleluia.
Nisi ego abiero, Paracletus non veniet:
Et dum assumptus fuero, mittam vobis eum. Alleluia.

(I ascend to my Father and to your Father, to my God and your God, alleluia. For if I go not, the Paraclete will not come to you; but if I go, I will send him to you. Alleluia.)

[3] Si quis diligit me

Antiphon for the magnificat in the second week after Pentecost Sunday (from John 14:23)

Si quis diligit me, sermonem meum servabit:
Et Pater meus diliget eum, et ad eum veniemus,
Et mansionem apud eum faciemus, alleluia.

(If any one love me, he will keep my word, and my Father will love him, and we will come to him, and will make our abode with him, alleluia.)

[4] Timete Dominum

Antiphon 7 for the third nocturn of All Saints, 1 November (from Psalm 33:10, 16)

Timete Dominum, omnes Sancti eius,
Quoniam nihil deest timentibus eum:
Ecce oculi Domini super iustos,
Et aures eius ad preces eorum, alleluia.

(Fear the Lord, all ye his saints, for there is no want to them that fear him. The eyes of the Lord are upon the just, and his ears unto their prayers, alleluia.)

[5] Exaudi Domine

Text unknown; cantus firmus from Josquin's chanson "Faut d'argent"

Exaudi Domine orationem nostram,
Et converte luctum nostrum in gaudium.
Spem in alium nunquam habuimus,
Praeterquam in te Domine.
Memento nostri, Domine, in tempore tribulationis nostrae.

(Hear our prayer, O Lord, and change our mourning into rejoicement. We never had trust in another more than in Thee, O Lord. Remember us, O Lord, in the time of our tribulation.)

[6] Derelinquat impius

Response for the first week of Lent (paraphrase of Joel 2:14, 13); cantus firmus text is verse 2 of the tract "Domine non secundum peccata nostra" for Ash Wednesday

[℟.] Derelinquat impius viam suam,
Et vir iniquus cogitationes suas,
Et revertatur ad Dominum,
Et miserebitur eius:
Quia benignus et misericors est,
Et praestabilis super malitia Domine Deus noster.

Cantus firmus: Adiuva nos, Deus.

([℟.] The wicked man must abandon the way of sin and the unjust man his evil thoughts; let him return to the Lord, who will be merciful. For the Lord our

God is gracious and merciful, and ready to repent of the evil.

Cantus firmus: Help us, O Lord.)

[7] Eripe me

Perhaps for Holy week (from Psalm 142:9–12, slightly altered)

[Prima pars]

Eripe me de inimicis meis, Domine,
Ad te confugi.
Doce me facere voluntatem tuam,
Quia Deus meus es tu.
Spiritus tuus bonus deducet me in terram rectam.
Propter nomen tuum, Domine, vivificabis me in ae-
    quitate tua.

Secunda pars

Educes de tribulatione animam meam,
Et in misericordia tua disperdes omnes inimicos
    meos,
Et perdes omnes qui tribulant animam meam,
Quoniam ego servus tuus sum.

(Deliver me from my enemies, O Lord, to thee have I fled: teach me to do thy will, for thou art my God. Thy good spirit shall lead me into the right land. For thy name's sake, O Lord, thou wilt quicken me in thy justice.

Thou wilt bring my soul out of trouble, and in thy mercy thou wilt destroy my enemies, and thou wilt cut off all them that afflict my soul, for I am thy servant.)

[8] Domine, si tu es

Response 4 in the Feast of Saints Peter and Paul, Apostles, 29 June (based on Matthew 14:28 and 31)

[℞.] Domine, si tu es, iube me venire ad te super
    aquas.
Et extendens manum apprehendit eum,
Et dixit Iesus: Modicae fidei, quare dubitasti?

([℞.] Lord, if it be thou, bid me come to thee upon the waters. And immediately Jesus stretching forth his hand took hold of him, and said to him: O thou of little faith, why didst thou doubt?)

[9] Domine ostende nobis Patrem

Antiphon at vespers and lauds for Saints Philip and James, 11 May (based on John 14:8–9)

Domine ostende nobis Patrem, et sufficit nobis, al-
    leluia.
Tanto tempore vobiscum sum, et non cognovistis me?

Philippe, qui videt me, videt et Patrem meum, alle-
    luia.

(Lord, show us the Father, and it is enough for us, alleluia. Have I been so long a time with you; and have you not known me? Philip, he that seeth me seeth the Father also, alleluia.)

[10] In principio erat Verbum

Text of responsories 11 and 12 for the Nativity of the Lord, 25 December (from John 1:1–14)

[Prima pars]

In principio erat Verbum,
Et Verbum erat apud Deum,
Et Deus erat Verbum.
Hoc erat in principio apud Deum.
Omnia per ipsum facta sunt:
Et sine ipso factum est nihil, quod factum est.
In ipso vita erat,
Et vita erat lux hominum:
Et lux in tenebris lucet,
Et tenebrae eam non comprehenderunt.
Fuit homo missus a Deo,
Cui nomen erat Ioannes.

Secunda pars

Hic venit in testimonium
Ut testimonium perhiberet de lumine,
Ut omnes crederent per illum.
Non erat ille lux,
Sed ut testimonium per hiberet de lumine.
Erat lux vera,
Quae illuminat omnem hominem
Venientem in hunc mundum.
In mundo erat, et mundus per ipsum factus est,
Et mundus eum non cognovit.

Tertia pars

In propria venit,
Et sui eum non receperunt.
Quotquot autem receperunt eum,
Dedit eis potestatem filios Dei fieri,
His qui credunt in nomine eius:
Qui non ex sanguinibus,
Neque ex voluntate carnis,
Neque ex voluntate viri,
Sed ex Deo nati sunt.
Et Verbum caro factum est,
Et habitavit in nobis:
Et vidimus gloriam eius,
Gloriam quasi unigeniti a Patre,
Plenum gratiae et veritatis.

(In the beginning was the Word, and the Word was with God, and the Word was God. The same was in the beginning with God. All things were made by him: and without him was made nothing that was made. In him was life, and the life was the light of men: and the light shineth in darkness, and the darkness did not comprehend it. There was a man sent from God, whose name was John.

This man came for a witness, to give testimony of the light, that all men might believe through him. He was not the light, but was to give testimony of the light. That was the true light, which enlighteneth every man that cometh into this world. He was in the world, and the world was made by him, and the world knew him not.

He came unto his own, and his own receiveth him not. But as many as received him, he gave them power to be made the sons of God, to them that believe in his name, who are born, not of blood, nor of the will of the flesh, nor of the will of man, but of God. And the Word was made flesh, and dwelt among us, and we saw his glory, the glory as it were of the only begotten of the Father, full of grace and truth.)

[11] O Rex gloriae

Set in the manner of a responsory and verse (with identical alleluia closings for the two *partes)*; part I appears as an antiphon at the magnificat of Sunday within the Octave of the Ascension (its text, in *LU* 853, the Breviary and Missal, is of unknown origin, while that of part II comes from Mark 16:15–16)

[Prima pars]

O Rex gloriae, Domine virtutum,
Qui triumphator hodie super omnes coelos ascendisti, alleluia,
Ne derelinquas nos orphanos:
Sed mitte promissum Patris in nos,
Spiritum veritatis, alleluia.

Secunda pars

Euntes in universum mundum predicate Evangelium omni creature, alleluia.
Qui crediderit, et baptisatus fuerit, salvus erit:
Qui vero non crediderit, condemnabitur, alleluia.

(O King of glory, Lord of hosts, who hast this day mounted in triumph above all the heavens, leave us not orphans, but send unto us the Promise of the Father, the Spirit of truth, alleluia.

Go ye into the whole world, and preach the gospel to every creature. He that believeth and is baptized, shall be saved: but he that believeth not shall be condemned, alleluia.)

[12] Heu michi, Domine

Responsory and Verse (variant) for the Faithful Departed, 2 November (the cantus firmus quotes Job 7:16, "Parce michi, Domine")

[℞.] Heu michi, Domine, quia peccavi nimis in vita mea:
Quid faciam, miser? ubi fugiam, nisi ad te, Deus meus?
Miserere mei, dum veneris in novissimo die.
[℣.] Anima mea turbata est valde, sed tu, Domine, Libera eam, dum veneris . . .

Cantus firmus: Parce michi, Domine.

([℞.] Alas for me, Lord! I have sinned exceedingly in my life. Wretch that I am, what shall I do? Where shall I fly but to you, my God? Have mercy on me when you come on the last day. [℣.] My soul is greatly troubled; come to its aid, O Lord, Have mercy on me . . .

Cantus firmus:.Spare me, O Lord.)

[13] Congregati sunt inimici nostri

Response 3 in the first Sunday of October

Congregati sunt inimici nostri,
Et gloriantur in virtute sua:
Contere fortitudinem illorum, Domine, et disperge illos:
Ut cognoscant quia non est alius qui pugnet pro nobis, nisi tu, Deus noster.

(Our enemies have gathered together, and they are boasting of their power. Destroy their strength, O Lord, and scatter them, that they may know that there is no one who fights for us but you, our God.)

[14] *Victimae paschali laudes*

Sequence for Easter Sunday

[Prima pars]

Victimae paschali laudes immolant Christiani.
Agnus redemit oves:
Christus innocens Patri reconciliavit peccatores.
Mors et vita duello conflixere mirando:
Dux vitae mortuus regnat vivus.
Dic nobis, Maria, quid vidisti in via?
Sepulchrum Christi viventis:
Et gloriam vidi resurgentis.

Secunda pars

Angelicos testes, sudarium, et vestes.
Surrexit Christus spes nostra:
Praecedet vos in Galileam.
Credendum est magis soli Mariae veraci,

Quam Iudaeorum turbae fallaci.
Scimus Christum surrexisse a mortuis vere:
Tu nobis, victor Rex, miserere.
Alleluia, alleluia.

(To the paschal Victim, let Christians dedicate their praises. The Lamb has redeemed the sheep; Christ the innocent one has reconciled the sinners with the Father. Death and life in a wondrous conflict strove. Life's Captain, who died, living, reigns. Tell us, O Mary, what thou sawest on thy way. The tomb of Christ the living, and the glory of his arising again, I saw.

The angelic witnesses, the veil, and the garments. Christ, my hope, has arisen: he goes before his own to Galilee. We must believe more in the light of Mary's veracity than in the crowd of erring Jews. We know that Christ has indeed risen from the dead: be merciful unto us, O victorious King. Alleluia, alleluia.)

[15] Omnes gentes attendite

Unknown text

Omnes gentes attendite ad tam pulchrum spectaculum;
Deo gratias agite, qui sic dilexit populum Mariae formam sumite,
Que virtutis est speculum, alleluia.

(All peoples pay heed to so lovely a spectacle; render thanks unto God, who so loved the people that he took his form from Mary, who is a mirror of virtue, alleluia.)

[16] Verbum caro factum est

Responsory and verse for the Nativity of Our Lord, 25 December (from John 1:14, 3)

[Prima pars]

[℟.] Verbum caro factum est,
Et habitavit in nobis:
Et vidimus gloriam eius,
Gloriam quasi unigeniti a Patre,
Plenum gratiae et veritatis.

Secunda pars

[℣.] Omnia per ipsum facta sunt,
Et sine ipso factum est nihil.
Et vidimus . . .

Tertia pars

Gloria Patri, et Filio, et Spiritui Sancto.
Et vidimus . . .

([℟.] And the Word was made flesh, and dwelt among us. And we saw his glory, the glory as it were of the only begotten of the Father, full of grace and truth.

[℣.] All things were made by Him, and without him was made nothing that was made. And we saw his glory . . .

Glory to the Father, the Son, and the Holy Spirit. And we saw his glory . . .)

[17] Nunc dimittis servum tuum

Tract: Canticle of Simeon, for the Purification of the Blessed Virgin Mary (from Luke 2:29–32)

Nunc dimittis servum tuum Domine,
Secundum verbum tuum in pace.
[℣.] Quia viderunt oculi mei salutare tuum.
[℣.] Quod parasti ante faciem omnium populorum.
[℣.] Lumen ad revelationem gentium,
Et gloriam plebis tuae Israël.

(Now thou dost dismiss thy servant, O Lord, according to thy word in peace. [℣.] Because my eyes have seen thy salvation. [℣.] Which thou hast prepared before the face of all peoples. [℣.] Light to the revelation of the Gentiles, and the glory of thy people Israel.)

[18] De fructu vitae

Unknown text; the cantus firmus, "Fiat cor meum et corpus meum immaculatum, ut non confundar," is from Psalm 118:80 (see Maillard's "Cantantibus Organis," motet *a 4* [RRMR 73] and antiphon 6 for matins for St. Cecilia)

De fructu vitae non gustabit cor tuum,
Nec sub umbra alarum mearum protegeris in aeternum.
Nam virgineum decus futuro sponso,
Immaculatum custodiam in seculum seculi.

Cantus firmus: Fiat cor meum et corpus meum immaculatum, ut non confundar.

(Your heart will not partake of the enjoyment of life, nor will it be shielded forever under the protection of my hosts. Truly, the groom is about to be the glory of the Virgin, the immaculate guardian through all generations.

Cantus firmus: Let my heart and my body be immaculate, that I may not be put to shame.)

[19] Fratres mei elongaverunt

Responsory 2 for Palm Sunday (paraphrasing Job 19:13–14); the annotation, "Me oportet minui, Illum autem crescere" (from John 3:30) designates a mensuration canon

[℞.] Fratres mei elongaverunt se a me,
Et noti mei quasi alieni, recesserunt a me.
[℣.] Dereliquerunt me proximi mei,
Et qui me noverunt quasi alieni, recesserunt a me.

([℞.] My kinsmen withdrew themselves from me, and my acquaintance like strangers have departed from me. [℣.] My kinsmen have forsaken me, and they that knew me have departed from me like strangers.

Cantus firmus: "He must increase, but I must decrease.")

[20] Ecce venit ad templum

Invitatory for the Purification of the Blessed Virgin Mary, matins, 2 February

Ecce venit ad templum sanctum suum Dominator Dominus:
Gaude et letare, Syon, occurens Deo tuo.

(Behold, the Lord and Ruler has come to his holy temple: rejoice and be glad in meeting your God, O Sion.)

[21] Vidit Dominus Petrum et Andream

Antiphons 1–3 for St. Andrew, Apostle, matins, 30 November (paraphrasing Mark 1:16–18)

Vidit Dominus Petrum et Andream, et vocavit eos.
Venite post me, dicit Dominus,
Faciam vos fieri piscatores hominum.
Relictis retibus suis, secuti sunt Dominum Redemptorem.
Alleluia.

(The Lord saw Peter and Andrew, and he called them. Come follow me, says the Lord, I will make you fishers of men. Leaving their nets, they followed the Lord and Redeemer. Alleluia.)

[22] Surrexit Dominus vere

Text for short responsory for Tuesday within the Octave of Easter, followed by Alleluia verse (Surrexit) for Easter Thursday (expanding on Luke 24:34); in the cantus firmus, the resolutio voice is a short responsory for Easter Sunday

[℞.] Surrexit Dominus vere, alleluia.
Et apparuit Simoni.
Surrexit Christus, qui creavit omnia:
Et misertus est humano generi.
Alleluia.

Resolutio: [℞.] Surrexit Dominus vere: alleluia.

([℞.] The Lord is risen indeed, alleluia, and hath appeared to Simon. Christ is risen, who created all things, and who had compassion upon the human race. Alleluia.)

[23] Decantabat populus Israël

Response for the third week after the Octave of Easter (based upon I Paralipomenon 15:28, 27); "Alleluia" lacking after "Israël" (line 1)

[℞.] Decantabat populus Israël,
Et universa multitudo Iacob canebat legitime:
Et David cum cantoribus cytharam percutiebat in domo Domini,
Et laudes Deo canebat, alleluia, alleluia.

(The people of Israel sang, and the whole multitude of the children of Jacob sang according to the law. And David accompanied the song on a harp in the house of the Lord, and sang alleluia, alleluia.)

[24] Estote ergo misericordes

Antiphon texts for the first Sunday after Pentecost (based on Luke 6:36–38)

Estote ergo misericordes,
Sicut et Pater vester misericors est.
Nolite iudicare, et non iudicabimini:
Nolite condemnare, et non condemnabimini.
Remittite, et remittetur vobis.
Date, et dabitur vobis.

(Be ye therefore merciful, as your Father is also merciful. Judge not, and you shall not be judged. Condemn not, and you shall not be condemned. Forgive, and you shall be forgiven. Give, and it shall be given to you.)

[25] In pace

From Psalms 4:9 and 131:4, with added material

[Prima pars]

In pace.

Secunda pars

Si dedero somnum oculis meis,
Et palpebris meis dormitationem.

Tertia pars

Gloria Patri, et Filio, et Spiritui Sancto.

(In peace.

If I shall give sleep to my eyes, or rest to my temples.

Glory be to the Father and to the Son and to the Holy Spirit.)

[26] Gaudent in caelis

Antiphon for the Common Commemoration of Saints, with a minor text variant at the end (instead of "exsultant sine fine," it is "regnant in aeternam")

Gaudent in caelis animae Sanctorum,
Qui Christi vestigia sunt secuti;
Et, quia pro eius amore sanguinem suum fuderunt,
Ideo cum Christo regnant in aeternum.

(The souls of the saints, who followed the footsteps of Christ, rejoice in heaven; and because they shed their blood for his love, therefore with Christ, they prevail throughout eternity.)

[27] Ave, Maria [I]

Marian antiphon (expansion of Luke 1:28)

Ave, Maria, Gratia plena:
Dominus tecum:
Benedicta tu in mulieribus,
Et benedictus fructus ventris tui, Iesus.
Amen.

(Hail Mary, full of grace, the Lord is with thee: blessed art thou among women, and blessed is the fruit of thy womb, Jesus. Amen.)

[28] Ave, Maria [II]

See [27].

[29] Deus, Deus meus

Offertory for the second Sunday after Easter (from Psalm 62:1–3)

Deus, Deus meus, ad te de luce vigilo.
Sitivit in te anima mea;
Quam multipliciter tibi caro mea!
In terra deserta, [et] invia, et inaquosa,
Sic in sancto apparui tibi,
Ut viderem virtutem tuam et gloriam tuam.

(O God, my God, to thee do I watch at break of day. For thee my soul hath thirsted; for thee my flesh, O how many ways! In a desert land, [and] where there is no way, and no water, so in the sanctuary have I come before thee, to see thy power and thy glory.)

[30] Ave, stella matutina

Antiphon for the Blessed Virgin Mary (text expansion)

[Prima pars]

Ave, stella matutina,
Mundi princeps et regina,
Virgo sola digna dici,
Inter tela inimici,
Clypeum pone salutis,
Tuae titulum virtutis.
Tu es enim virga Iesse,
In qua Deus fecit esse,
Aaron amygdalum,
Mundi tollens scandalum.

Secunda pars

Tu es area compluta,
Caelesti rore imbuta,
Sicco tamen vellere:
Tu nos in hoc carcere,
Solare propicia,
Dei plena gratia,
O mater Dei electa,
Esto nobis via recta,
Ad aeterna gaudia,
Ubi pax est et gloria,
Et nos semper aure pia,
Dulcis exaudi Maria.

(Hail, O star of the morning, Princess and Queen of the world; alone worthy to be called a virgin; among the weapons of the adversary, place your shield for safety, the evidence of your excellence. You are indeed the staff of Jesse, the rod of Aaron, who take away the temptation of the world.

You are watered earth, imbued with celestial dew; therefore pluck us out of this prison, anew, filled with the grace of the Lord. O chosen mother of God, be to us the right path to eternal joy, where peace is glory, and hear us always with a compassionate ear, sweet Mary.)

[31] Tota pulchra es

Antiphon in honor of the Blessed Virgin Mary (variant of Song of Songs 4:7–9, 11)

Tota pulchra es amica mea:
Et macula non est in te.
Veni de Libano sponsa mea veni:
Vulnerasti cor meum, soror mea, sponsa:
Favus distillans, labia tua sponsa:
Mel et lac sub lingua tua:
Et odor vestimentorum tuorum, sicut odor thuris.

(Thou art all fair, O my love, and there is not a spot in thee. Come from Libanus, my spouse; thou hast wounded my heart, O my sister, my spouse. Thy lips distill nectar, my bride, and honey and milk are under thy tongue. And the smell of thy garments is like the smell of frankincense.)

[32] O crux benedicta

Text unknown (perhaps an antiphon for the Exaltation of the Holy Cross, 14 September)

O crux benedicta,
Quia in te pependit Salvator mundi,
Et in te triumphavit Rex angelorum:
Per quam salvati et liberati sumus.

(O blessed Cross, on you did hang the Savior of the world, and on you did triumph the King of the angels, by which we are saved and made free.)

[33] Regina coeli

Marian antiphon for Sunday at compline

[Prima pars]

Regina coeli laetare, alleluia:
Quia quem meruisti portare, alleluia:

Secunda pars

Resurrexit, sicut dixit, alleluia:
Ora pro nobis Deum, alleluia.

(Queen of heaven, rejoice, alleluia, for he whom you were chosen to bear, alleluia, has risen as he said, alleluia! Pray God for us, alleluia.)

[34] Inviolata, integra

Sequence in honor of the Blessed Virgin Mary

Inviolata, integra, et casta es Maria:
Quae es effecta fulgida coeli porta.
O Mater alma Christi carissima:
Suscipe pia laudum praeconia.
Nostra ut pura pectora sint et corpora.
Te nunc flagitant devota corda et ora:
Tu das per precata dulcisona:
Nobis concedas veniam per secula.
O benigna! O Regina! O Maria!
Quae sola inviolata permansisti.
Cantus firmus: Ave, Maria, gratia plena.

(Inviolate, perfect, and pure are you, O Mary, who are made the glittering gate of heaven. O merciful, beloved Mother of Christ: receive, O gracious one, the proclamations of praise. Our devoted hearts long for you, that our bodies and souls be cleansed. You give, through sweet prayers, you grant us eternal favor. O kind one, O Queen, O Mary, who alone remained inviolate.
Cantus firmus: Hail, Mary, full of grace.)

[35] Diffusa est gratia

Responsory, Common of Virgins and Holy Women not Virgins (from Psalm 44:3, 5)

[℞.] Diffusa est gratia in labiis tuis,
Propterea benedixit te Deus in aeternum.
[℣.] Specie tua et pulchritudine tua
Intende, prospere procede, et regna.
Propterea . . .

([℞.] Grace is poured abroad in thy lips; therefore hath God blessed thee for ever. [℣.] With thy comeliness and thy beauty set out, proceed prosperously, and reign. Therefore hath God . . .)

[36] Stemmata maiorum

Text unknown

Stemmata maiorum fulgent clarissima praesul.
Fultaque nobilibus stat domus altatuis.
Moribus insignis nulli pietate secundus,
Tu superas sacra religione numen.
Te duce pauperiem norunt deppellere multi
Est tua pauperibus spesque salusque domus.

(The coat of arms of your elders shines brightly. Your lofty house stands above others, supported by your noble kinsmen, In excellent morals and piety you are second to none, You overcome the [secular] will by holy religion. Under your leadership many have learnt to drive away [spiritual?] poverty; your house is hope and salvation to the poor.)

[37] Puer natus est

Introit for the third mass of the Nativity (from Isaias 9:6)

Puer natus est nobis,
Et filius datus est nobis:
Cuius imperium super humerum eius:
Et vocabitur nomen eius,
Magni consilii Angelus.

(A Child is born to us, and a Son is given to us: and the government is upon his shoulder: and his name shall be called the Angel of Great Counsel.)

[38] Assumpta est Maria

Variant of antiphon at second vespers, 15 August

Assumpta est Maria in coelum:
Gaudent Angeli, laudantes benedicunt Dominum.
Elegit eam Deus, et praeelegit eam Deus:
Habitare facit eam in tabernaculo suo.

(Mary has been taken up into heaven! The angels are rejoicing; praising they bless the Lord. God has chosen her beforehand. He makes her dwell in his tabernacle.)

[39] Hodie Maria virgo

Conflation of the antiphon "Hodie" and the versicle and response "Exaltata est," for the Assumption of the Blessed Virgin Mary, 15 August, first and second vespers

Hodie Maria Virgo caelos ascendit:
Gaudete, quia cum Christo regnat in aeternum.

Exaltata est sancta Dei Genetrix.
Super choros Angelorum ad caelestia regna.

(This day the Virgin Mary ascended into heaven; rejoice, for she reigns with Christ forever. The holy Mother of God is lifted up on high, above the choirs of angels into the kingdom of heaven.)

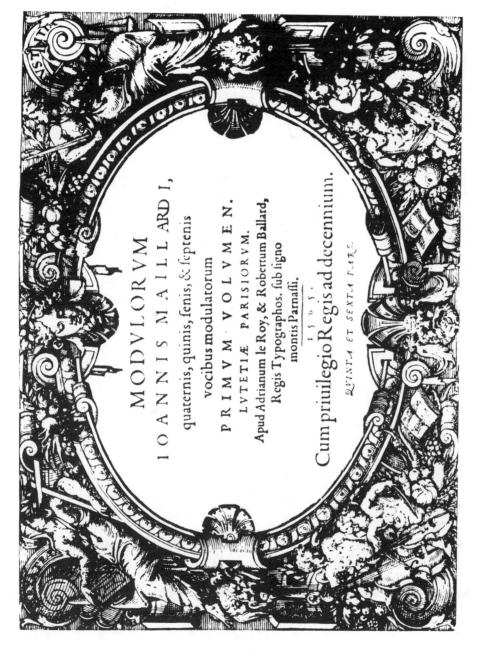

Plate 1. Jean Maillard, *Modulorum Ioannis Maillardi . . . primum volumen* (Paris: Adrian Le Roy and Robert Ballard, 1565 [=LRB 96]), Quinta et Sexta Pars, fol. 1r, title page. Chicago, The Newberry Library, Case VM 2099 .L1 K39. (Courtesy The Newberry Library)

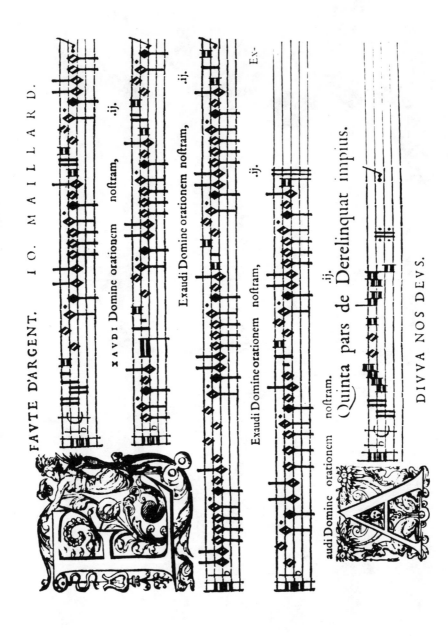

Plate 2. LRB 96, Quinta et Sexta Pars, fol. 4v, "Exaudi Domine" and "Derelinquat impius" ([5] and [6] in this edition). Chicago, The Newberry Library, Case VM 2099 .L1 K39. (Courtesy The Newberry Library)

Plate 3. LRB 96, Quinta et Sexta Pars, fol. 16r, "Vidit Dominus" ([21] in this edition). Chicago, The Newberry Library, Case VM 2099 .L1 K39. (Courtesy The Newberry Library)

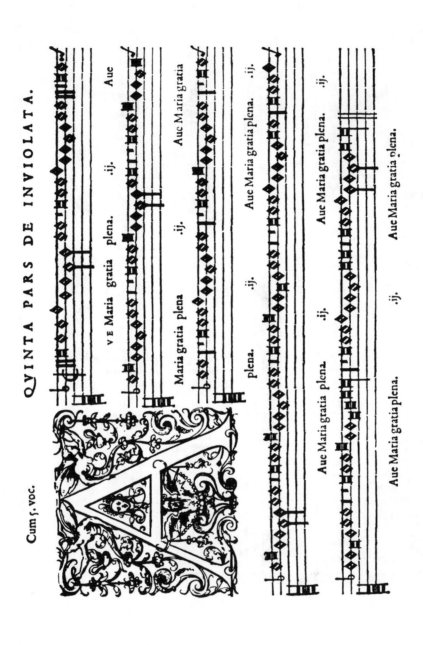

Plate 4. Jean Maillard, *Modulorum Ioannis Maillardi . . . secundum volumen* (Paris: Adrian Le Roy and Robert Ballard, 1565 [= LRB 97]), Quinta et Sexta Pars, fol. 7v, "Inviolata, integra" ([34] in this edition). Chicago, The Newberry Library, Case VM 2099 .L1 K39. (Courtesy The Newberry Library)

Plate 5. LRB 96, Quinta et Sexta Pars, fol. 13r, "De fructu vitae" ([18] in this edition). Chicago, The Newberry Library, Case VM 2099 .L1 K39. (Courtesy The Newberry Library)

MOTETS *A* 5 FROM LRB 96

[1] Laudate Dominum, omnes gentes

4

6

[2] Ascendo ad Patrem meum

8

12

fu- - e- ro,⟩ mit- tam vo- bis _____ e-

mit- tam vo- bis e- um, mit- tam vo- bis, mit- tam vo-

-tam vo- bis e- um, ⟨mit- tam vo- bis e-

-sum- ptus fu- e- ro,⟩ _____ mit- tam vo- bis e-

mit- tam vo- bis e- - um,

-um, mit- tam vo- bis _____ e- um.

-bis e- um, ⟨mit- tam vo- bis _____ e-

- um,⟩ mit- tam vo- bis e- - um. Al-

-um, ⟨mit- - tam vo- bis e- um,⟩ mit- tam vo- bis _____

mit- tam vo- bis, mit- - tam vo- bis e- um. _____

Al- le- lu- ia, al- le- lu-

- um.⟩ _____ Al- le- lu- ia, ⟨al- le- lu-

- le- lu- ia, ⟨al- le- lu- ia,⟩ al- - le- lu-

e- um. Al- le- lu- ia, ⟨al- le- lu- ia,⟩ al-

Al- le- lu- ia, ⟨al- le- lu- ia,⟩

13

14

[3] Si quis diligit me

16

[4] Timete Dominum

22

24

[5] Exaudi Domine

28

[6] Derelinquat impius

[7] Eripe me

38

40

[8] Domine, si tu es

48

[9] Domine ostende nobis Patrem

20
Do- - mi- ne o- sten- - de no- bis Pa-
o- sten- de no- bis Pa- - trem, et suf-
-trem, Do- - mi- ne o- sten- de no- bis
-trem,
- - trem, o- sten- - de no- bis Pa-
25
- trem, et suf- fi- cit
-fi- cit no- - bis, et
Pa- - trem, et suf- fi- cit
et suf- fi- cit no- - bis,
- trem, et suf- fi- cit, et suf- fi- cit no-
30
no- - - bis, al- le- lu- ia, al-
suf- fi- cit no- - bis, al- le- lu- ia,
no- - bis, al- le- lu-
et suf- fi- cit no- - bis, al-
- - bis, al- le- lu- ia,

[10] In principio erat Verbum

56

58

60

62

64

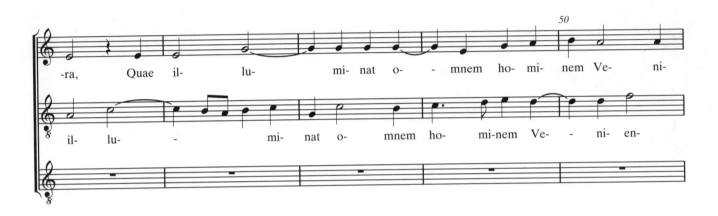

72

Et vi- di- mus glo- ri- am e- ius, Glo- ri- am qua-

Et vi- di- mus glo- ri- am e- ius, Glo- ri- am qua-

-mus glo- ri- am e- ius, _____ Glo-

e- ius, _____ Glo- ri- am qua- si,

Glo- ri- am qua- si,

- si _____ u- ni- ge- ni-

-si u- ni- ge- ni- ti _____ à Pa-

-ri- am qua- si u- ni- ge- ni- ti à

⟨glo- ri- am qua- si⟩

glo- ⟨ri- am qua- si⟩ u- ni- ge- ni- ti à Pa-

-ti à Pa- tre, Ple- num gra- ti- ae et ve- ri-

-tre, Ple- num gra- ti- ae, ple- num gra- ti- ae et

Pa- tre, Ple- num gra- ti- ae et

Ple- num gra- ti- ae, _____ ple- num gra- ti- ae

-tre, Ple- num gra- ti- ae _____

[11] O Rex gloriae

82

[12] Heu michi, Domine

94

[13] Congregati sunt inimici nostri

96

[14] Victimae paschali laudes

104

106

108

[15] Omnes gentes attendite

114

118

[16] Verbum caro factum est

122

124

126

Tertia pars

Superius

Glo- ri- a Pa- tri, glo-

Contratenor

Glo- ri- a Pa- tri, et Fi- li- o,

Quinta Pars

Glo- ri- a Pa- tri, et Fi- li- o, et Fi-

Tenor

Bassus

-ri- a Pa- tri, et Fi- li- o, et Spi- ri- tu-

⟨glo- ri- a Pa- tri, et Fi- li- o,⟩ et Spi-

-li- o, glo- ri- a Pa- tri, et Fi- li- o,

-i San- cto, et Spi- ri- tu- i San-

-ri- tu- i San- cto, et Spi- ri- tu- i, et

et Spi- ri- tu- i San- cto, ⟨et Spi-

[17] Nunc dimittis servum tuum

134

[18] De fructu vitae